AP '11

The MAILBOX®

The Education Center®

Big Book of Monthly Reproducibles

grade **1**

W9-AHV-133

- Includes more than **120** pages for independent practice

- Builds key language arts and math skills

- Features popular holidays and seasonal themes

> Our favorite seasonal and holiday pages from our popular Monthly Reproducibles series and *Teacher's Helper*® magazine

Managing Editor: Krystle Short Jones

Editorial Team: Becky S. Andrews, Diane Badden, Kimberley Bruck, Karen A. Brudnak, Pierce Foster, Tazmen Hansen, Marsha Heim, Lori Z. Henry, Kitty Lowrance, Jennifer Nunn, Mark Rainey, Hope Rodgers, Rebecca Saunders, Rachael Traylor, Sharon M. Tresino

www.themailbox.com

©2010 The Mailbox® Books
All rights reserved.
ISBN10 #1-56234-941-4 • ISBN13 #978-1-56234-941-7

Printed in the United States
10 9 8 7 6 5 4 3 2 1

HPS215487

Table of Contents

September

Back-to-School
Uppercase and lowercase letters............. 5
Skip-counting 6
Addition 7

Labor Day
Writing sentences 8
Classification 9

National Grandparents Day
Classification.. 10

Apples
Writing the alphabet 11
Short vowel *a* 12
Counting.. 13
Ordering numbers 14

Constitution Day
Reading comprehension 15

October

Fall
Lowercase and uppercase letters 16
Initial consonants 17
Opposites.. 18
Patterning... 19
Greater than and less than 20
Addition... 21
Word problems.. 22

Fire Prevention Week
ABC order 23
Reading comprehension 24

Columbus Day
Reading comprehension 25
True and false 26

Harvest
Initial consonants 27
Initial consonants 28

Spiders
Reading comprehension 29
Final consonants.................................... 30

Halloween
Ending punctuation 31
Skip-counting 32
Sets.. 33
Money 34

November

Election Day
Greater than and less than 35

Turkeys
Long and short vowels 36
Addition facts 37
Skip-counting 38
Money 39
Telling time 40

Colonial Kids
Short vowels 41
Addition... 42

Native Americans
Subtraction.. 43
Patterning.. 44

Thanksgiving
Short vowels 45
Long vowels 46
Sequencing 47
Money 48

December

Hanukkah
Vocabulary 49
Measurement 50

Gingerbread
Long vowels 51
Beginning blends 52

Christmas
Long vowels 53
ABC order 54
Skip-counting 55
Sorting solid shapes 56
Graphing 57

Kwanzaa
Punctuation 58
Word problems 59

January

New Year
Writing sentences 60
Following directions 61

Martin Luther King Day
Vocabulary 62
Reading for details 63

Winter
ABC order 64
Addition and subtraction 65
Graphing 66
Temperature 67

Penguins
Predicting outcomes 68
Graphing 69
Addition and subtraction 70
Fact families 71

100th Day of School
Place value 72

February

Chinese New Year
Telling time 73

Black History Month
Reading comprehension 74

National Children's Dental Health Month
Beginning blends 75
Compound words.................................. 76

Groundhog Day
Contractions 77
Reading comprehension 78
Reading a chart.................................... 79

Valentine's Day
Beginning blends 80
Graphing 81
Addition and subtraction 82
Telling time 83

Presidents' Day
Table of contents................................. 84
Three-column addition 85

March

Wind
Fractions 86

Lions and Lambs
Long vowels.. 87
Contractions... 88
Calendar 89
Subtraction... 90

St. Patrick's Day
Digraphs.................................... 91
Fact and opinion 92
Telling time 93
Money 94
Addition and subtraction 95

Spring
Rhyming... 96
Journal prompts 97
Fact families.. 98

April

April Fools' Day
ABC order 99
Geometric patterns 100

Jelly Beans
Graphing 101

Bunnies
Digraphs.. 102
Reading comprehension 103
Addition and subtraction 104

Earth Day
Contractions.. 105
Plurals 106

Raindrops
Graphing 107
Addition 108

Rainbows
Equal parts.. 109
Greater than and less than 110

Frogs
Antonyms 111
Synonyms 112
Addition and subtraction 113

May

Baseball
Syllabication.. 114
Reading a chart...................................... 115

Cinco de Mayo
Word problems.. 116

Flowers
Long *o*.. 117
Sequencing 118
Missing addends 119

Bees
Complete sentences 120
Predicting outcomes 121
Identifying nouns................................... 122
Addition 123

Memorial Day
Reading comprehension 124
Three-column addition 125

End of the Year
Writing reflections 126
Word problems...................................... 127

Summer

Addition... 128

Homework Time

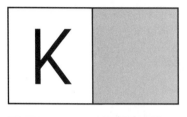Cut.

Glue.

Write.

K

N

T

O

F

Z _ _ _ _ _ _ _

M

H

D

R

f	z	n	m	h
d	k	t	o	r

Mr. Caterpillar's Classroom

Count.

Write.

A.	_5_ crayons
B.	___ pencils
C.	___ paintbrushes
D.	___ rulers
E.	___ glue bottles

Sorting Supplies

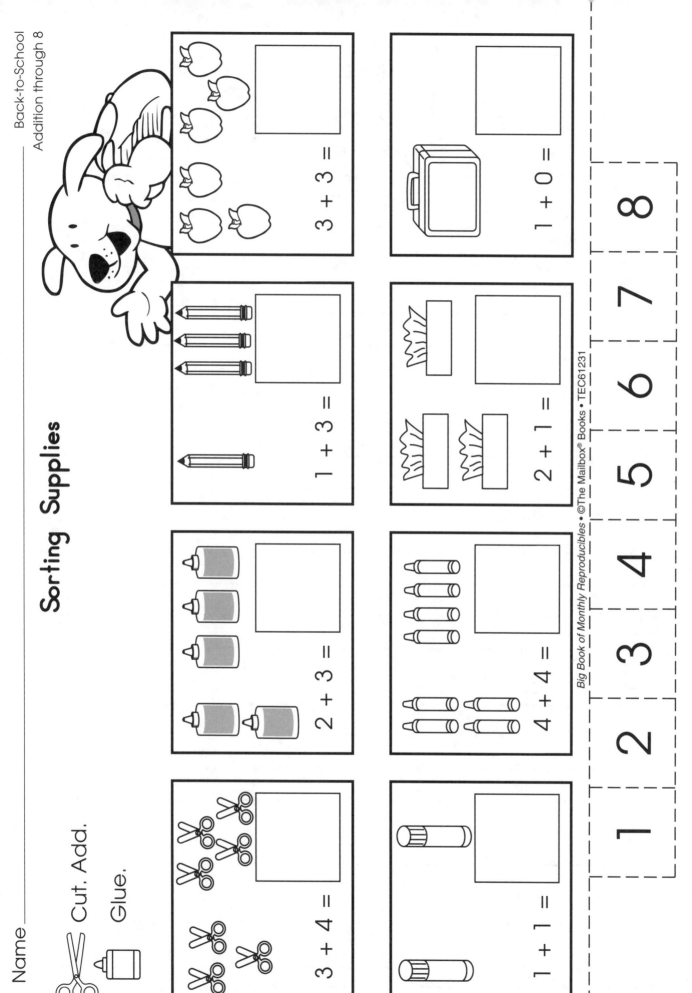

Cut. Add.
Glue.

3 + 3 =

1 + 3 =

2 + 3 =

3 + 4 =

1 + 0 =

2 + 1 =

4 + 4 =

1 + 1 =

1 2 3 4 5 6 7 8

Big Book of Monthly Reproducibles • ©The Mailbox® Books • TEC61231

Future Plans

✏️ Write.

When I grow up, I want to be

_____

- -

_____

I would like this job because

_____

- -

_____

- -

_____

- -

_____

I will need to learn

_____

- -

_____

- -

_____

I will wear

_____

- -

Tools of the Trade

Write.

spoon	brush	hose	car
book	saw	X-ray	comb

painter	brush

firefighter	

hairstylist	

police officer	

builder	

teacher	

baker	

doctor	

Kitchen Clutter!
Grandma and Grandpa need help cleaning up the kitchen.

Draw an **x** if it does not belong.

Cut.

Glue to match each set.

Apple Alphabet

Fill in Johnny Appleseed's alphabet.

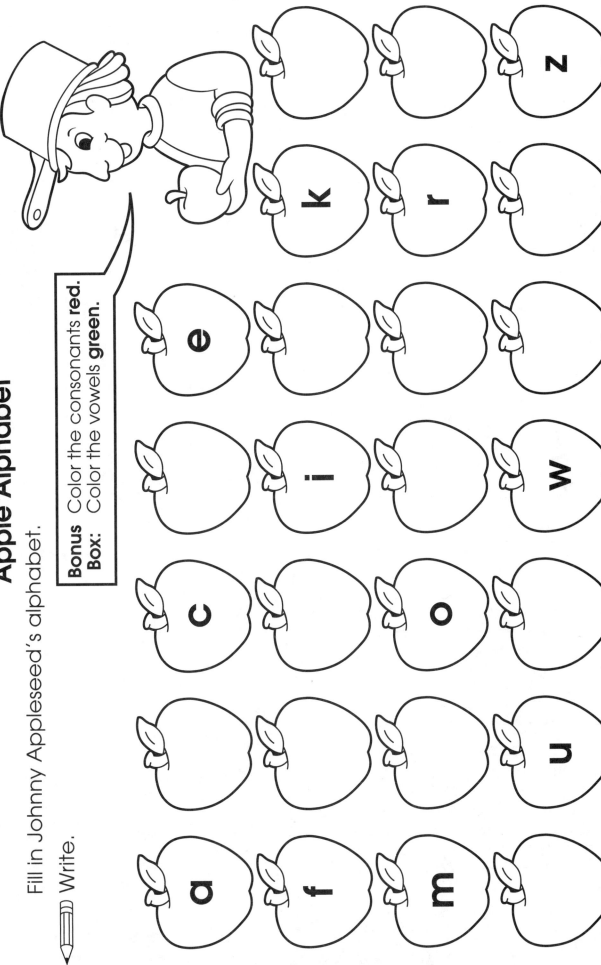

Bonus Color the consonants **red.**
Box: Color the vowels **green.**

Write.

Mouse Sneaks Johnny's Snack

Say the name of each picture.

Lightly color the picture red if you hear the short sound of **a**.

Bonus Box: Draw a different picture with the short sound of **a** on the back of this sheet.

A Lot of Apples!

Count.

Write.

By the Bushel

 Write the missing numbers.

A.  1 2 ___ ___ 5 ___

B.  9 ___ ___ 12 13 ___

C.  7 ___ ___ 10 ___ 12

D.  12 ___ 14 ___ 16 ___

E.  ___ 16 17 ___ 19 ___

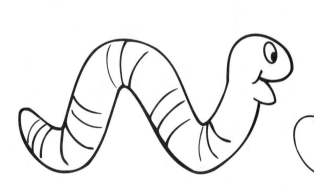

Bonus Box: Write the numbers from 10 to 20 on the back of this paper.

Big Book of Monthly Reproducibles • ©The Mailbox® Books • TEC61231

The United States Constitution

Read.

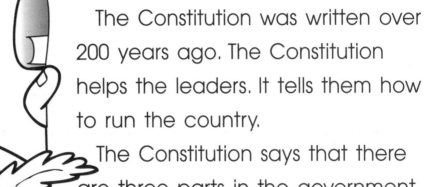

The Constitution was written over 200 years ago. The Constitution helps the leaders. It tells them how to run the country.

The Constitution says that there are three parts in the government. One part makes the laws. One part makes sure that people follow the laws. The last part tells what the laws mean.

The Constitution also tells people what their rights are. It is an important paper.

Color the 🪶 blue if the sentence is **true.**

Color the 🪶 red if the sentence is **not true.**

1. The Constitution helps leaders run the country.

2. It was written a long time ago.

3. There are four parts in the U.S. government.

4. The Constitution gives people rights.

Lots of Leaves!

✏ Write the matching lowercase letter.

B   M   W

F   G   N   J

E   A   Q   D

R   Y   P   K

T

H   I

Beyond "Be-leaf"

Color by the code.

Color Code

c

d

l

p

r

Bonus Box: On the back of this sheet, draw things that begin with *l*—such as a leaf.

Autumn Opposites

Look at the pictures.
Match the opposites.

✂ Cut. 🗴 Glue.

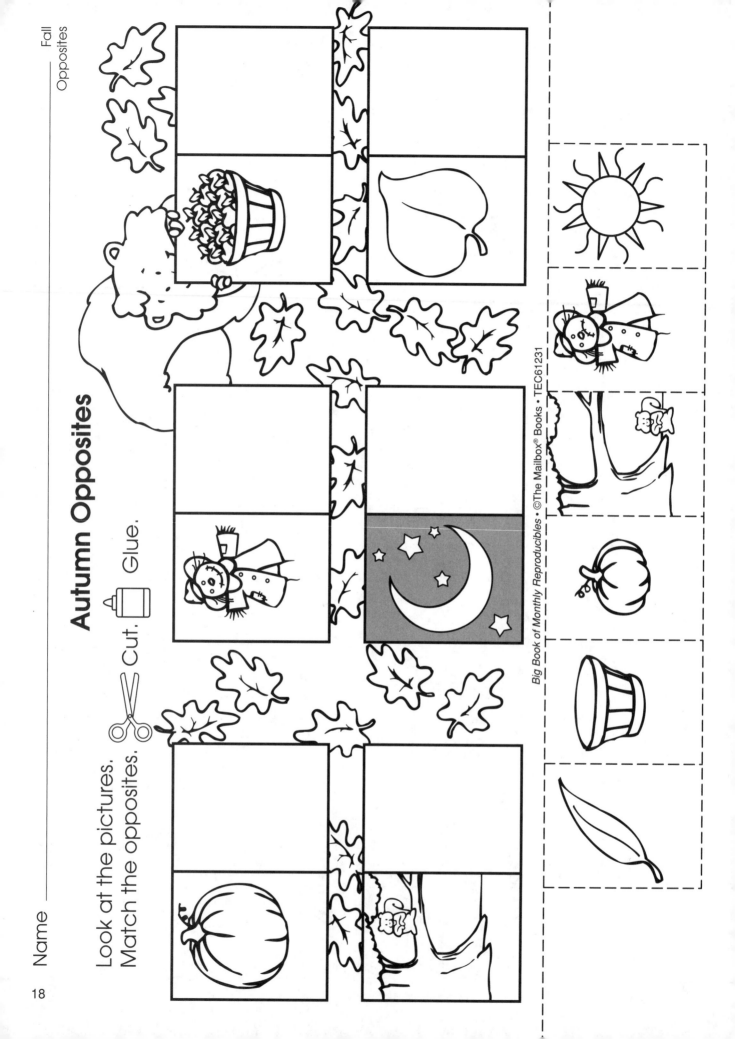

Big Book of Monthly Reproducibles • ©The Mailbox® Books • TEC61231

Barnyard Buddies

Cut and glue to complete each pattern.

     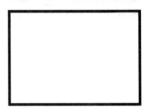

  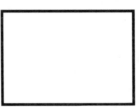  

   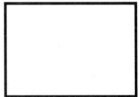

   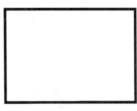  

  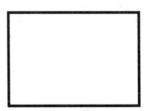  

19

Go, Team, Go!

Less Than

4

7

8

Greater Than

2

< means **less than.**

> means **greater than.**

Look at the numbers below.
Write < or > in each circle.

4 ◯ 2	8 ◯ 5	3 ◯ 4
6 ◯ 5	2 ◯ 7	9 ◯ 5
5 ◯ 8	6 ◯ 3	8 ◯ 7
7 ◯ 9	2 ◯ 0	1 ◯ 6

Big Book of Monthly Reproducibles • ©The Mailbox® Books • TEC61231

Acorns Aplenty!

Add.

A.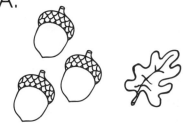

3 + 1 = _____

B.

1 + 0 = _____

C.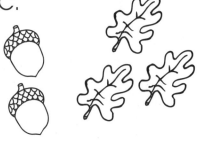

2 + 3 = _____

D.

4 + 2 = _____

E.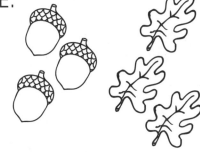

3 + 3 = _____

F.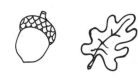

1 + 1 = _____

G.

3 + 0 = _____

H.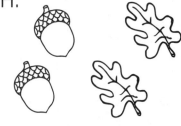

2 + 2 = _____

I.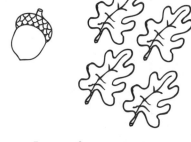

1 + 4 = _____

J.

5 + 1 = _____

Gathering Acorns

✂ Cut. Read.

✏ Write the number sentence.
Use the counters to help you.

C. Sally has **1** acorn.
Sam gives her **9** more.
How many acorns does
she have in all?

____ + ____ = ____
acorns

D. Sam sees **3** acorns.
Sally sees **5** acorns.
How many acorns do
they see in all?

____ + ____ = ____
acorns

E. Sam finds **4** acorns.
Sally finds **3** acorns.
How many acorns do
they find in all?

____ + ____ = ____
acorns

A. Sam has **2** acorns.
Sally has **3** acorns.
How many acorns do
they have in all?

____ + ____ = ____
acorns

B. Sally hides **7** acorns.
Sam hides **2** acorns.
How many acorns do
they hide in all?

____ + ____ = ____
acorns

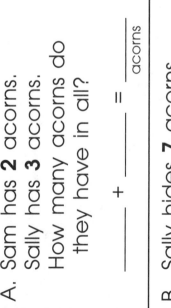
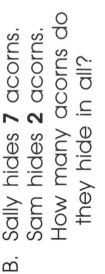

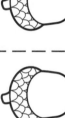

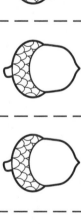

Wet Words

Write each set of words in ABC order.

stop
drop
roll
crawl

1.

2.

3.

4.

1.

2.

3.

4.

smoke
fire
truck
hose

Be Fire Smart!

Read.
Choose a word.
Write.

Do you know what to do if there is a fire?

_____

1. Stay _____ the smoke.

under
ugly

_____

2. Feel the _____ to see if it is hot.

drip
door

_____

3. Go to a _____ place.

safe
sing

_____

4. Do not go back _____.

idea
inside

_____

5. Call 911 for _____.

happy
help

Write a fire safety rule.

_____

_____

_____

Big Book of Monthly Reproducibles • ©The Mailbox® Books • TEC61231

A New Land

Read.

Christopher Columbus was a sailor. He hoped to find a new way to get from Spain to Asia. Columbus and his men sailed three ships across the sea. The trip was long. Sometimes it rained. One day they saw land. Columbus thought they had made it to Asia. He was wrong. He had really found a different land.

Circle the best word for each sentence.

Write each word on the line.

1. Columbus was a _____.
   sailor   doctor

2. Columbus and his men sailed _____ ships.
   four   three

3. The trip was _____.
   long   short

4. Sometimes it _____.
   snowed   rained

5. Columbus had found a different _____.
   ship   land

Name _____

Across the Sea

Read.

Christopher Columbus lived a long time ago. He liked to sail. He liked to find new things. He had a plan to explore the sea. He sailed across the sea with three ships. He sailed for many days. Then he saw land that was new to him. We call the land America!

Read each sentence below.

Color the circle green if the sentence is **true.**

Color the circle red if the sentence is **not true.**

◯ 1. Columbus lived many years ago.

◯ 2. He liked to ride on ships.

◯ 3. He sailed with two ships.

◯ 4. His trip was short.

◯ 5. He sailed to America.

Bonus Box: Look at the sentences that are not true. Change the sentences to make them true.

26   Big Book of Monthly Reproducibles • ©The Mailbox® Books • TEC61231

Name _____

Harvest

Initial consonants: *b, f, m, s, t*

Clever Crows

Cut and glue to match.

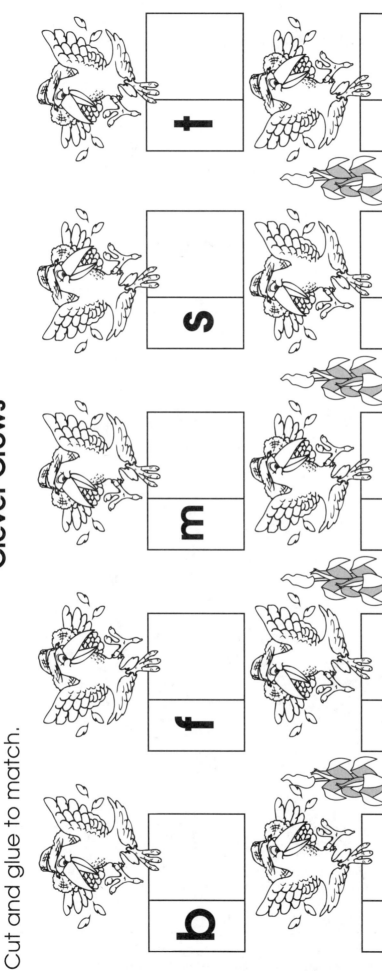

b	**f**	**m**	**s**	**t**

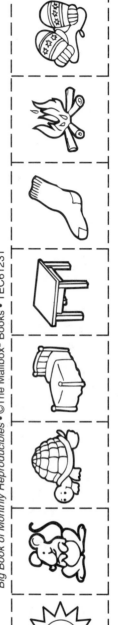

Bonus Box: *Bird* begins with *b*. On the back of this sheet, draw things that begin with *b*.

Big Book of Monthly Reproducibles • ©The Mailbox® Books • TEC61231

27

What's in the Pumpkin Patch?

Write the letter that begins each picture name.

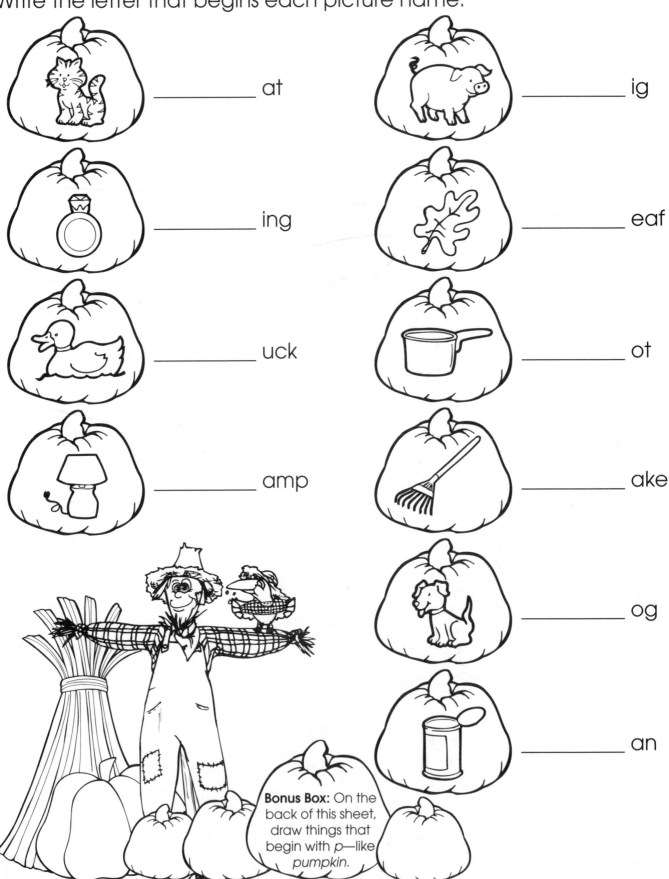

_____ at

_____ ig

_____ ing

_____ eaf

_____ uck

_____ ot

_____ amp

_____ ake

_____ og

_____ an

Bonus Box: On the back of this sheet, draw things that begin with *p*—like *pumpkin.*

See the Spider!

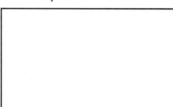

Read.
Find a picture for each bold word.
Cut and glue.
Draw the spider to match each sentence.

1. See the spider by the **cat**.

2. See the spider on the **hat**.

3. See the spider in the **house**.

4. See the spider under the **mouse**.

5. See the spider above the **car**.

6. See the spider in the **jar**.

Big Book of Monthly Reproducibles • ©The Mailbox® Books • TEC61231

Web Words

Say each picture name.
Listen for each ending sound.
Color by the code.

Color Code:

d = red

g = blue

n = green

p = yellow

t = purple

Party Plans

✏️ Write **.** , **?** , or **!** in each box.

🖍️ Color a matching pumpkin.

1. When will the Halloween party start ☐

2. It will start in one hour ☐

3. We will get a lot of candy ☐

4. Look at Ann's costume ☐

5. What a great costume ☐

6. What will Sam be for Halloween ☐

7. He will be a clown ☐

8. Boy, Halloween is fun ☐

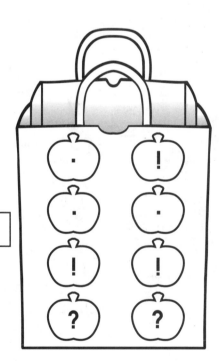

Bonus Box: On the back of this paper, write a different sentence about Halloween.
Remember to write a **.** , **?** , or **!** at the end.

Candy Corn Counting

 Cut.

Count by tens or fives.

 Glue.

A.
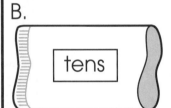 tens   10   30   40   60

B.
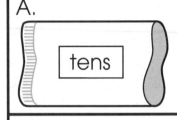 tens   40   50   70   80

C.
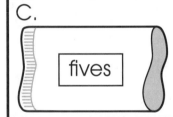 fives   5   15   20   30

D.
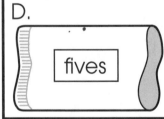 fives   55   60   65   80

Bonus Box: On the back of this paper, write the numbers from 10 to 100 by tens.

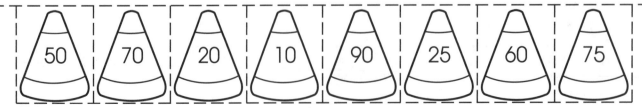

50   70   20   10   90   25   60   75

Trick-or-Treat Totals

Name _____

Draw.
Add.

$$\begin{array}{r}3\\+3\\\hline\end{array}$$

$$\begin{array}{r}2\\+6\\\hline\end{array}$$

$$\begin{array}{r}3\\+4\\\hline\end{array}$$

$$\begin{array}{r}5\\+1\\\hline\end{array}$$

$$\begin{array}{r}8\\+0\\\hline\end{array}$$

$$\begin{array}{r}2\\+5\\\hline\end{array}$$

$$\begin{array}{r}4\\+4\\\hline\end{array}$$

$$\begin{array}{r}4\\+2\\\hline\end{array}$$

$$\begin{array}{r}2\\+3\\\hline\end{array}$$

$$\begin{array}{r}1\\+7\\\hline\end{array}$$

$$\begin{array}{r}3\\+5\\\hline\end{array}$$

Sweet Treats

Cut.

Glue to match the amount of money.

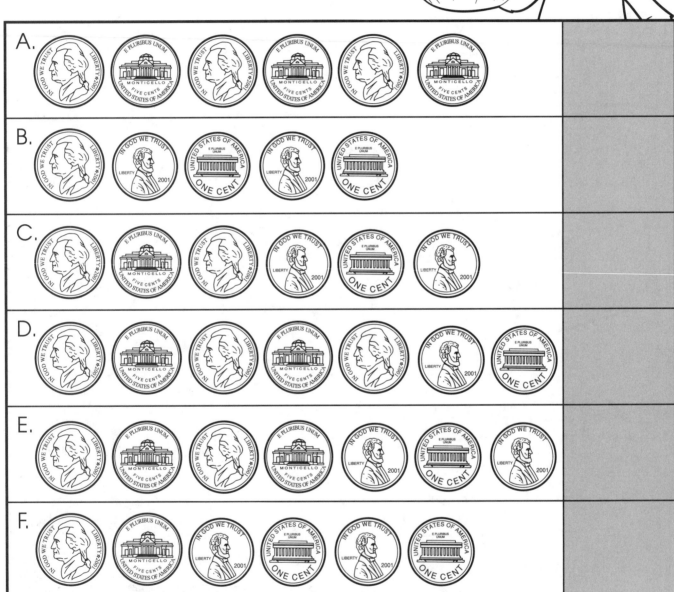

14¢

9¢

30¢

23¢

27¢

18¢

The Votes Are In!

Count the votes in each box.
Write the numbers on the lines.
Circle the bigger number in each box.

Ballot Box

Vote
For Your
Favorite
Pet

_____   _____

Vote
For Your
Favorite
Food

_____   _____

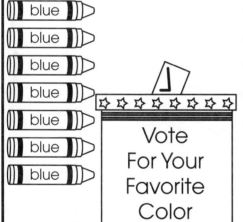

Vote
For Your
Favorite
Color

_____   _____

Vote
For Your
Favorite
Season

_____   _____

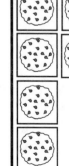

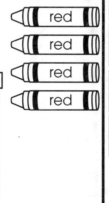

Vote
For Your
Favorite
Treat

_____   _____

Vote
For Your
Favorite
Sport

_____   _____

Turkey Mix-Up

Tom Turkey is cooking dinner.
His food got all mixed up!
Help him sort long vowels
from short vowels.

Remember!
Long vowels say
their names.

Cut and glue.

short vowels	long vowels

ham	rice	grapes	lime	milk	crab
cake	fish	pie	egg	cheese	bun

Name _____

Busy Baker

Add.

Color by the code.

$$\begin{array}{r} 7 \\ +2 \\ \hline \end{array}$$

$$\begin{array}{r} 6 \\ +4 \\ \hline \end{array}$$

$$\begin{array}{r} 4 \\ +4 \\ \hline \end{array}$$

$$\begin{array}{r} 1 \\ +8 \\ \hline \end{array}$$

$$\begin{array}{r} 3 \\ +7 \\ \hline \end{array}$$

$$\begin{array}{r} 5 \\ +4 \\ \hline \end{array}$$

$$\begin{array}{r} 5 \\ +5 \\ \hline \end{array}$$

$$\begin{array}{r} 7 \\ +1 \\ \hline \end{array}$$

$$\begin{array}{r} 2 \\ +7 \\ \hline \end{array}$$

$$\begin{array}{r} 7 \\ +3 \\ \hline \end{array}$$

I ♥ pies!

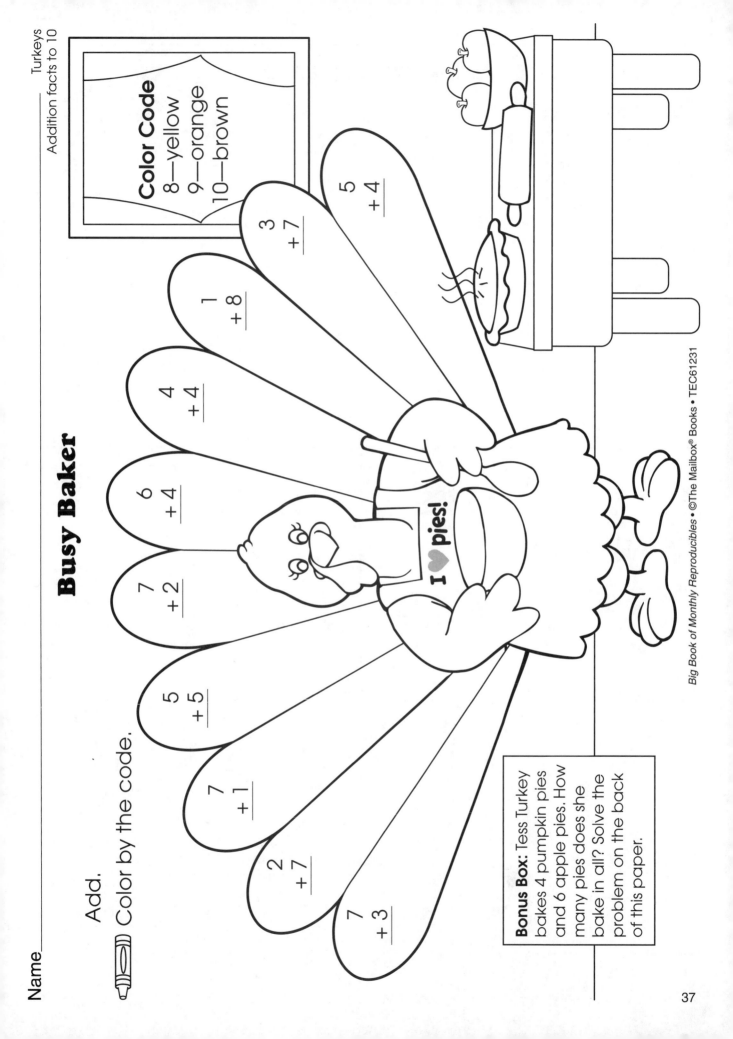

Bonus Box: Tess Turkey bakes 4 pumpkin pies and 6 apple pies. How many pies does she bake in all? Solve the problem on the back of this paper.

Name _____

Gobbler Groupings

Each turkey has ten feathers.
How many feathers are in each group?
Count by tens. Cut and glue.

Bonus Box: On the back of this sheet, write the tens from 10 to 100.

1 ten = 10 feathers	2 tens = 20 feathers
3 tens = 30 feathers	4 tens = 40 feathers
5 tens = 50 feathers	6 tens = 60 feathers
7 tens = 70 feathers	8 tens = 80 feathers
9 tens = 90 feathers	

Name_____

Busy Shopping Day

 Cut.

 Glue.

30¢	50¢	40¢

20¢	15¢	10¢

Big Book of Monthly Reproducibles • ©The Mailbox® Books • TEC61231

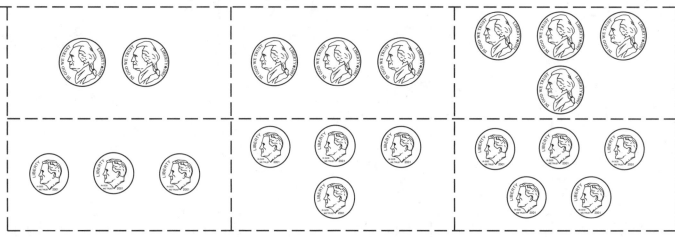

Turkey Time

Color the box that shows the time.

| 2:00 | 11:00 |

| 3:00 | 6:00 |

| 4:00 | 9:00 |

| 5:00 | 12:00 |

| 8:00 | 1:00 |

| 7:00 | 3:00 |

| 4:00 | 10:00 |

| 4:00 | 8:00 |

| 10:00 | 9:00 |

| 12:00 | 11:00 |

| 7:00 | 2:00 |

| 1:00 | 6:00 |

Colonial Comforts

These are things some colonial kids had in their homes.
Say each picture name.
Cut and glue to match.

| bed | doll | pot | dish | mug |
| chest | log | hat | wig | socks |

Name _____

Colonial Hornbook

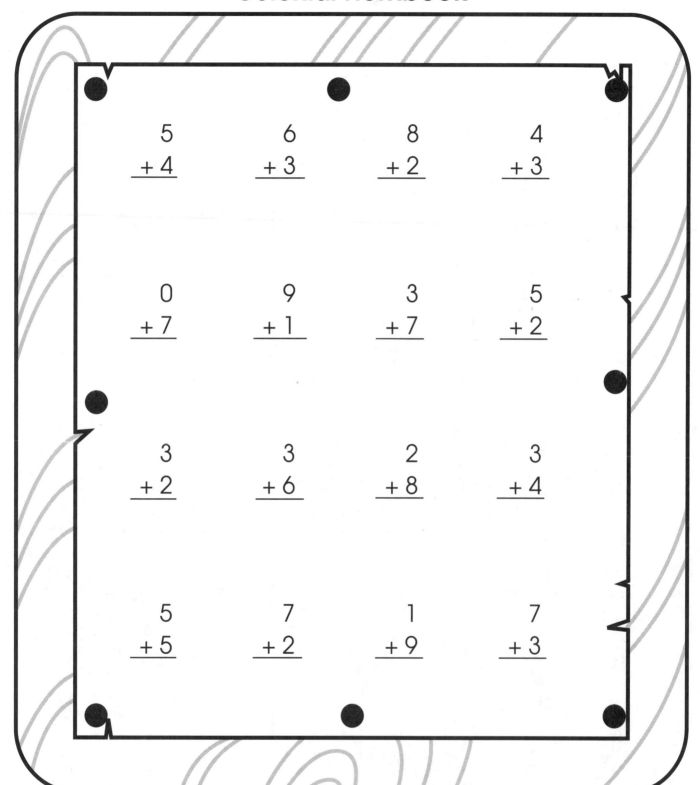

5 + 4	6 + 3	8 + 2	4 + 3
0 + 7	9 + 1	3 + 7	5 + 2
3 + 2	3 + 6	2 + 8	3 + 4
5 + 5	7 + 2	1 + 9	7 + 3

Bonus Box: Colonial kids used a one-page hornbook to learn their alphabet and numbers. On the back of this sheet, write the alphabet and the numbers 1–10.

Name_____

A Happy Harvest

Subtract.
Cross out foods in each basket to solve.
Write.

8 − 2 = ____

7 − 4 = ____

6 − 3 = ____

5 − 3 = ____

8 − 5 = ____

5 − 4 = ____

6 − 2 = ____

7 − 6 = ____

8 − 6 = ____

6 − 4 = ____

Bonus Box: There were 8 apples in the basket. Sam used 3 apples to make a pie. How many apples were left in the basket?

Beautiful Beadwork

Many Native Americans made designs with beads.
Sometimes they made patterns.
Draw to finish each pattern.

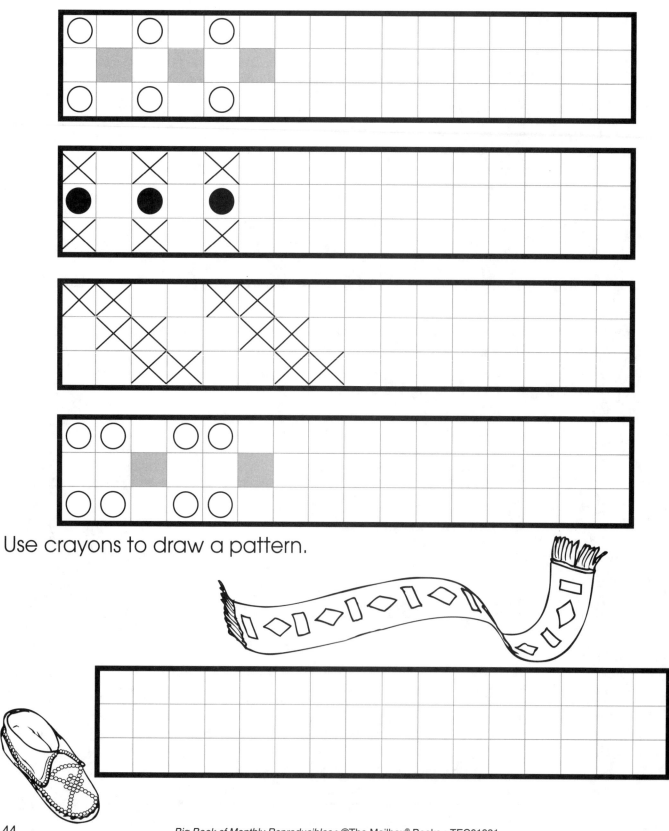

Use crayons to draw a pattern.

Feasting Friends

Color the pictures in each row
   that have the vowel sound shown.

ă	
ĕ	
ĭ	
ŏ	
ŭ	

Pilgrim Pie

Say each picture name.
Circle the vowel.
Color each box by the code.

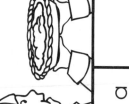

a e u	 a e i	 a o u	e i o
e i a	e i u	a e o	 a o u
a i u	 u e a	 o i u	u o e

Color Code: a = blue   e = green   i = red   o = yellow   u = orange

Name _____

Thanksgiving Dinner

✂ Cut.
Glue the pictures in order.

1	2	3	4

Big Book of Monthly Reproducibles •©The Mailbox® Books • TEC61231

Then we all sit at
the table.

First, we cook dinner.

Finally, we clean up.

Next, we eat the
food.

47

Pilgrim Pockets

Count the coins in each pocket.
Circle the correct amount.

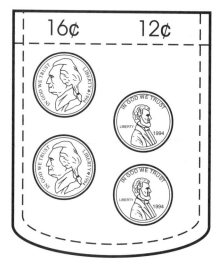

16¢   12¢

22¢   13¢

18¢   24¢

23¢   25¢

20¢   15¢

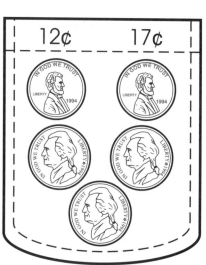

12¢   17¢

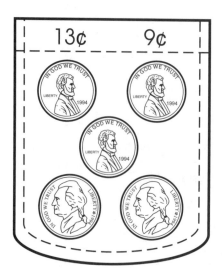

13¢   9¢

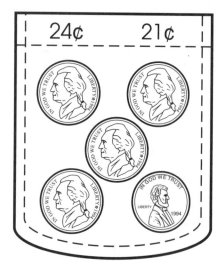

24¢   21¢

Name _____

Hanukkah Fun!

✂ Cut. 🖌 Glue to complete the sentences.

1. Sara lights the _____ in the menorah.

2. There are nine candles in the _____.

3. Ben helps Mom cook _____.

4. Who will spin the _____ first?

5. Sara wins lots of gold _____!

6. They open one _____ each night.

gift

coins

latkes

candles

dreidel

menorah

Light Height

Use a ruler.

Measure.

✂ Cut. Glue.

6 cm | 8 cm | 10 cm | 11 cm | 3 cm | 12 cm | 7 cm | 4 cm

A Sweet Surprise

Color by the code.

(Hint: You will not color three words.)

Color Code			
ā—red	ē—blue	ī—brown	ō—green

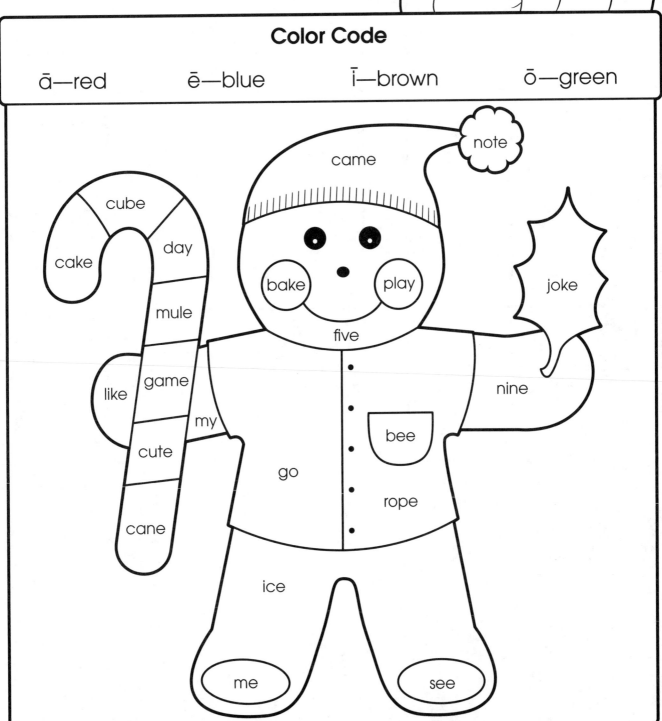

Bonus Box: On the back of this sheet, write the words that you did not color. Write a sentence with each word.

Gingerbread Boy Blends

Cut and glue to show each beginning blend.

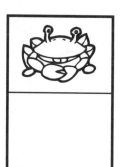

cr	cr	br	fr	fr	gr
cr	br	br	fr	gr	gr

Elves at Work

Cut out the pictures.
One of these things will help the elves.
Glue it to the X.
Glue the rest of the pictures below the matching vowel sound.

$\bar{a}$ $\bar{e}$ $\bar{i}$

Name _____

Christmas Greetings

✏ Write each group of words in ABC order.

✂ Cut.

🖊 Glue a stamp to match each group of words.

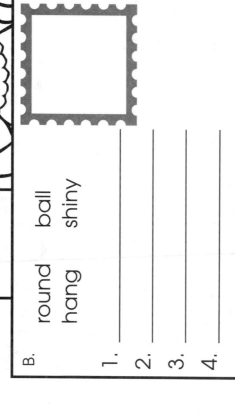

A.

cookie   sweet
brown   man

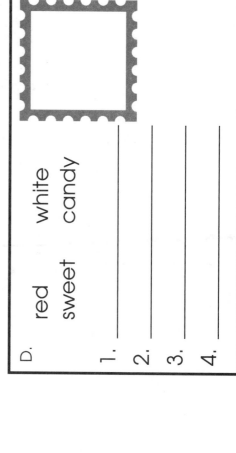

B.

round   ball
hang   shiny

1. _____
2. _____
3. _____
4. _____

1. _____
2. _____
3. _____
4. _____

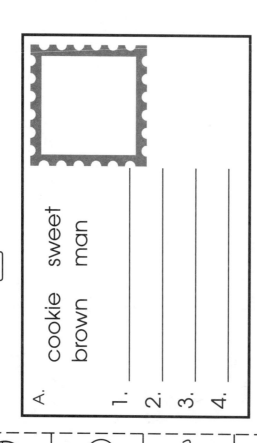

C.

green   tree
star   branch

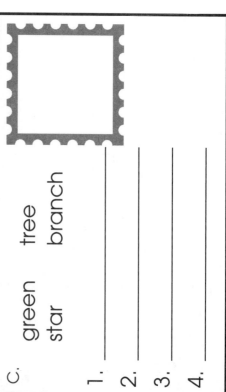

D.

red   white
sweet   candy

1. _____
2. _____
3. _____
4. _____

1. _____
2. _____
3. _____
4. _____

Big Book of Monthly Reproducibles • ©The Mailbox® Books • TEC61231

Jingle Bell Count

Count the bells in the boxes.
Write the numbers by fives to 100.

Gifts Galore!

Read and do.

1. Color each shape that will stack.

     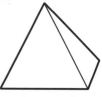

2. Color each shape that will roll.

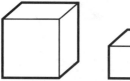 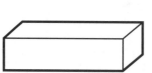 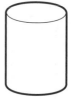 

3. Color each shape that will slide.

  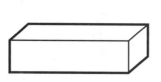 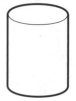 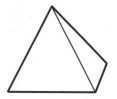

4. Color each shape that will roll and stack.

   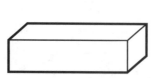

5. Color each shape that will slide and stack.

  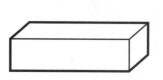 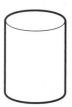 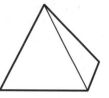

What's Your Favorite Color?

Color. Cut.

Glue to make a graph.

Colorful Christmas Lights

green					
red					
blue					

Use the graph to answer the questions.

1. How many green lights are there? _____

2. How many red lights are there? _____

3. How many blue lights and green lights are there in all? _____

Big Book of Monthly Reproducibles • ©The Mailbox® Books • TEC61231

red	blue	green	red	red	green
blue	red	green	red	blue	green

Name _____

Kwanzaa Lights

Read each sentence.

Write **.** or **?** in each ☐.

Color.

1. Kwanzaa is celebrated for seven days ☐

2. What will we eat for the feast ☐

3. When should we light the candles ☐

4. Let's dance to African music ☐

5. The colors for Kwanzaa are red, black, and green ☐

6. Fruits are shared during Kwanzaa ☐

7. Did you read stories about African people ☐

8. Where should I put the gifts ☐

Name_____

Harvest Gifts

Read.

Write the math sentence.

A. 12 apples are in the bowl.
6 apples are eaten.
How many apples are left
in the bowl?

_____ – _____ = _____
      apples

B. 5 pears are in the bowl.
4 pears are on the table.
How many pears are there
in all?

_____ + _____ = _____
      pears

C. 9 ears of corn are yellow.
3 ears of corn are white.
How many ears of corn are
there in all?

_____ + _____ = _____
      ears of corn

D. 10 grapes are in the bunch.
8 grapes fall off.
How many grapes are left in
the bunch?

_____ – _____ = _____
      grapes

E. 7 bananas are in the bowl.
4 apples are in the bowl.
How many pieces of fruit
are there in all?

_____ + _____ = _____
      pieces of fruit

F. 11 oranges are in the bowl.
6 oranges are eaten.
How many oranges are left
in the bowl?

_____ – _____ = _____
      oranges

Happy Kwanzaa!

Bonus Box: There are 5 pears and 7 apples in the bowl. How many pieces of fruit are there in all? On the back of this paper, write a math sentence to show your answer.

Ringing Resolutions

Write a resolution on each bell.

This is my
resolution for
school.

_____

_____

_____

This is my
resolution for
home.

_____

_____

_____

This is my
resolution for
myself.

_____

_____

_____

Big Book of Monthly Reproducibles • ©The Mailbox® Books • TEC61231

What a Party!

Read and do.

☐ Color the bell yellow.

☐ Draw hats on the dogs.

☐ Color the hats blue.

☐ Draw 4 balloons.

☐ Draw red dots on the balloons.

☐ Draw hands on the clock to show that it is 12:00.

Remembering His Dream

Read.

☆ At one time, all people were not ☆ treated the same. Dr. King did not think that was **fair.** But he did not want people to fight. He wanted **peace.** He wanted **respect** for everyone.

Complete the sentence.

_____

I show respect for others by _____

_____

_____

_____

_____

_____

_____

_____

Bonus Box: On the back of this paper, use the word **fair** in a sentence. Draw a picture to go with your sentence.

A Loving Leader

Read.
Complete each sentence.

Dr. Martin Luther King Jr. was a good leader. He loved to give speeches. He asked people to live peacefully. He helped change laws that were not fair. He wanted all people to be treated the same. He helped make things better for everyone!

1. Dr. King was a good _____.

2. Dr. King wanted people to live _____.

3. He helped change _____ that were not fair.

4. Dr. King wanted everyone to be treated the _____.

5. He helped make things _____ for _____!

Name _____

Winter Windows

Read the words in each box.
Write 1, 2, and 3 to show ABC order.

_____ track	_____ winter	_____ nose
_____ snow	_____ zipper	_____ red
_____ van	_____ yellow	_____ mitten
_____ sled	_____ melt	_____ cold
_____ push	_____ coat	_____ dog
_____ ice	_____ fan	_____ girl

Bonus Box: On the back of this sheet, write a winter story. Use the words with a "1" beside them in your story.

_____ boot	_____ jump
_____ chill	_____ hat
_____ sock	_____ tree

 Big Book of Monthly Reproducibles • ©The Mailbox® Books • TEC61231

Snowflake Surprise

Add or subtract.
If an answer is 10, color the space blue.

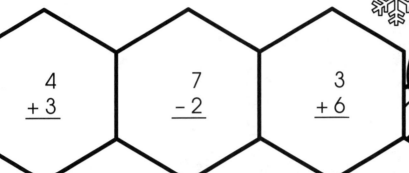

4
+ 3

7
− 2

3
+ 6

3
+ 5

10
− 3

4
+ 4

9
− 3

5
+ 5

7
+ 3

10
− 5

4
+ 6

9
− 5

2
+ 8

10
− 6

10
− 0

1
+ 9

8
− 6

5
+ 4

8
− 5

10
− 7

Name_____

Let It Snow!

Color one box on the graph for each
item you find in this winter picture.

snowperson	hat	mitten	snowflake	button

Bonus Box: Draw yourself in the picture. Be sure you are dressed for winter.

Winter Weather

32°F is freezing.
Look at the thermometers.
Write an answer for each question below.

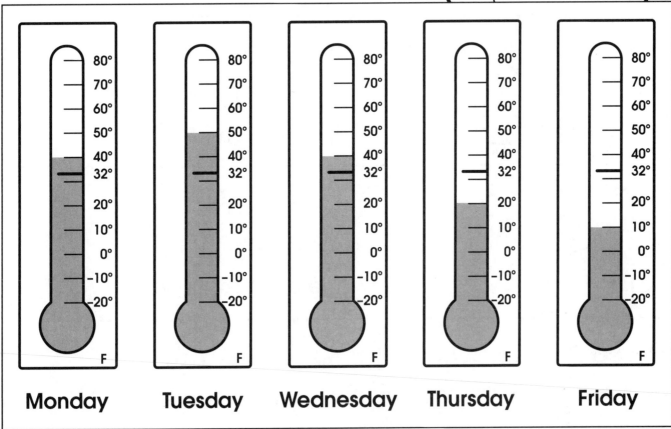

| **Monday** | **Tuesday** | **Wednesday** | **Thursday** | **Friday** |

1. Which day was the coldest? _____

2. Which two days had the same temperature?
   _____ and _____

3. On which day was the temperature 50°F? _____

4. On which two days was the temperature below freezing?
   _____ and _____

5. Which day had the warmest temperature? _____

Bonus Box: On the back of this sheet, write about a time when the temperature was below freezing.

Predictable Penguins

Look at each picture.
Read the sentences.
Color the circle that tells what the penguin will do next.

	○ The penguin will eat. ○ The penguin will jump. ○ The penguin will fall.
	○ The penguin will run. ○ The penguin will swim. ○ The penguin will sleep.
	○ The penguin will sing. ○ The penguin will swim. ○ The penguin will skate.
	○ The penguin will play ball. ○ The penguin will fly. ○ The penguin will read.
	○ The penguin will skip. ○ The penguin will walk. ○ The penguin will slide.

Big Book of Monthly Reproducibles • ©The Mailbox® Books • TEC61231

A Penguin's Prey

Color one box on the graph for each animal you find in the picture.

Add. Use the graph.

fish
+
squid
_____
[ ]

[ ]

[ ]

krill
+
squid
_____
[ ]

[ ]

[ ]

fish
+
krill
_____
[ ]

[ ]

[ ]

fish   [ ]
+
squid [ ]
+
krill   [ ]

Penguin Pal

Add or subtract.
Color a matching penguin part as you find each answer.

6 + 4	10 − 8	9 − 5	3 + 7

10 − 2	2 + 8	8 − 5	4 + 5

10
− 9

5
+ 5

9
− 4

10
− 7

8
− 4

Bonus Box: Add the numbers on the penguin's scarf. What is the sum?

All in the Family

Find each missing number. Write it in the box.

$6 + \boxed{} = 10$

$4 + 6 = \boxed{}$

$\boxed{} - 4 = 6$

$10 - 6 = \boxed{}$

$7 + 2 = \boxed{}$

$2 + \boxed{} = 9$

$9 - 2 = \boxed{}$

$\boxed{} - 7 = 2$

$\boxed{} + 3 = 11$

$3 + 8 = \boxed{}$

$11 - \boxed{} = 8$

$11 - 8 = \boxed{}$

$5 + 4 = \boxed{}$

$4 + 5 = \boxed{}$

$\boxed{} - 4 = 5$

$9 - \boxed{} = 4$

$7 + 5 = \boxed{}$

$\boxed{} + 7 = 12$

$\boxed{} - 5 = 7$

$12 - 7 = \boxed{}$

Bonus Box: On the back of this sheet, write two addition and two subtraction problems for the fact family **8, 2, 10.**

Hooray for the 100th Day

Read the key.

✏️ Write how many tens and ones.

✏️ Write each number.

Key

🍕 = 1 slice

PIZZA = 10 slices in a box

1.
PIZZA PIZZA PIZZA
🍕 🍕

☐

___ tens ___ ones

2.
PIZZA PIZZA PIZZA PIZZA
🍕 🍕
🍕 🍕

☐

___ tens ___ ones

3.
PIZZA PIZZA PIZZA PIZZA PIZZA
🍕

☐

___ tens ___ ones

4.
🍕 🍕
🍕 🍕
🍕 🍕
PIZZA

☐

___ tens ___ ones

5.
PIZZA PIZZA PIZZA PIZZA PIZZA
PIZZA PIZZA PIZZA PIZZA PIZZA

☐

___ tens ___ ones

6.
PIZZA PIZZA
🍕 🍕 🍕
🍕 🍕 🍕

☐

___ tens ___ ones

7.
PIZZA PIZZA PIZZA
🍕

☐

___ tens ___ ones

8.
PIZZA PIZZA
🍕 🍕 🍕
🍕 🍕 🍕
🍕

☐

___ tens ___ ones

9.
PIZZA PIZZA PIZZA PIZZA PIZZA

☐

___ tens ___ ones

Bonus Box: Find the problem with 100 and then color the matching boxes.

Name_____

Time to Celebrate!

Write each time.

A.

Time to clean.

:

B.

Time to eat.

:

C.

Time for a
parade.

:

D.

Time to give
gifts.

:

E.

Time to make
a lantern.

:

F.

Time for
fireworks.

:

Hard Work Pays!

Read.

Complete each sentence.

Jesse Owens

When Jesse Owens was a young man, he had a dream. He wanted to run at the Olympic games. He trained for many years. His dream came true in 1936. He went to the games and won four gold medals. He won three of the medals for races. He won one medal for the broad jump. His hard work paid off!

1. Jesse Owens dreamed of running at the Olympic

   _____.

2. He _____ for a long time.

3. He went to the games in _____.

4. Jesse won _____ gold medals.

5. He won most of the medals for _____.

6. He won _____ medal for the broad jump.

Tooth Tips

Read the sentences.
Write the word to complete each sentence.

_____

1. _____ after every meal.
   Blush   Brush   Brag

_____

2. Eat healthful _____.
   snaps   snacks   sleds

_____

3. Use dental _____ each day.
   flower   flag   floss

_____

4. Have a dentist _____ your teeth.
   clean   clam   crop

_____

5. Show off your _____.
   smart   smile   slide

Write each beginning blend.

_____

_____ ush

_____

_____ oss

Brushing Up!

Cut and glue to make compound words.

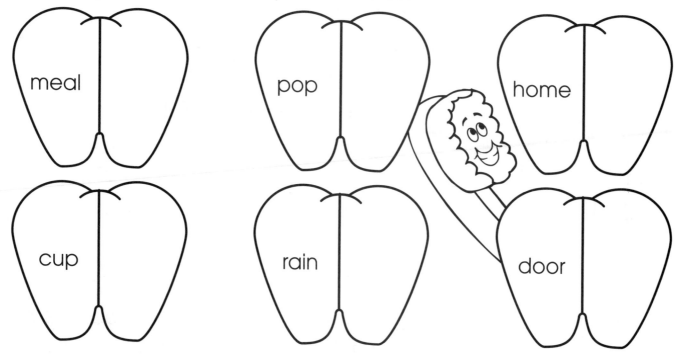

meal

pop

home

cup

rain

door

Write to make compound words. Use the word bank.

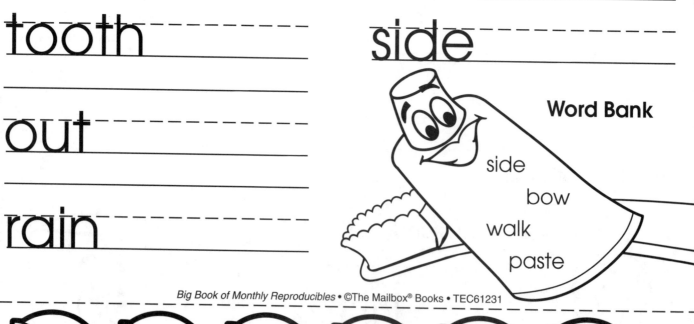

tooth

out

rain

side

Word Bank

side
bow
walk
paste

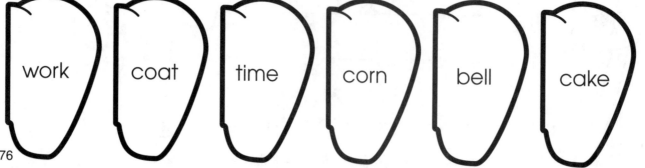

work   coat   time   corn   bell   cake

A Hat for Mr. Groundhog

Cut. Match. Glue.

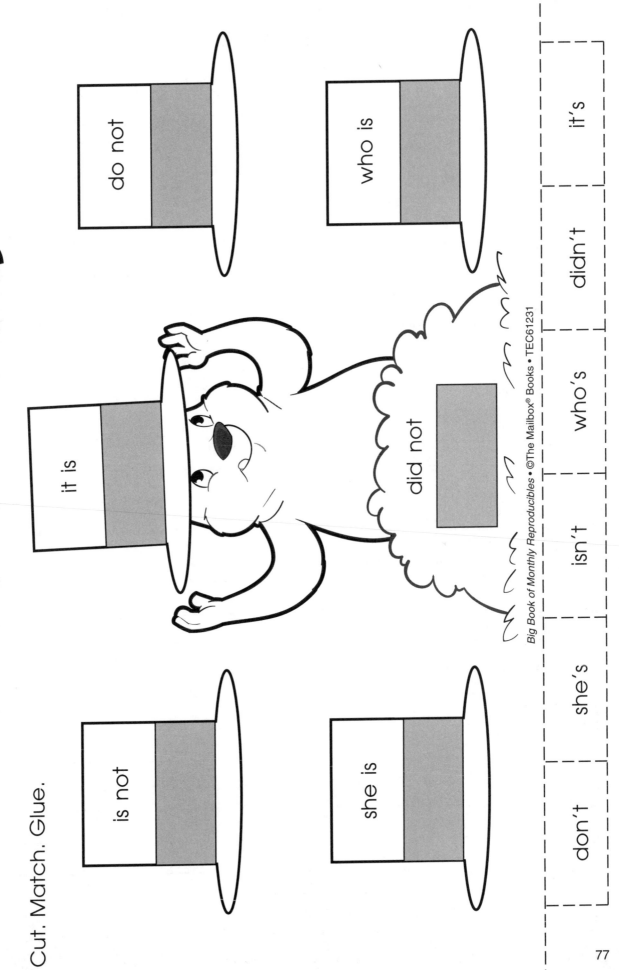

do not

who is

it is

did not

is not

she is

it's   didn't   who's   isn't   she's   don't

Big Book of Monthly Reproducibles • ©The Mailbox® Books • TEC61231

Shadow Story

Read the story.

Was it time for spring? All the animals were waiting to find out. Where was Mr. Groundhog? He would decide if spring would come or if there would be more winter.

All the animals called for Mr. Groundhog. Soon he poked his nose through the dirt. Mr. Groundhog pulled himself from the hole. He did not see his shadow. "Hooray!" the animals shouted. "It is time for spring!"

Answer the questions.

1. Who would decide if spring would start?

_____

_____

2. Where did Mr. Groundhog live?

_____

_____

3. What was Mr. Groundhog looking for?

_____

_____

4. How did the animals feel at the end of the story?

_____

_____

Bonus Box: Draw clouds in the sky to hide the sun.

Big Book of Monthly Reproducibles • ©The Mailbox® Books • TEC61231

Amazing Animals

Use the chart to answer the questions.

Animal	Body Covering	Food
groundhog	fur	plants
bird	feathers	bugs, meat, seeds, or fruit
frog	wet skin	bugs

1. What does a groundhog eat? _____

2. What covers a groundhog? _____

3. How many animals are on the chart? _____

4. Which one has wet skin? _____

5. Which one does not eat bugs? _____

6. Which one eats bugs and has feathers? _____

Bonus Box: Use the chart to find one thing that is different between a groundhog and a frog. Write your answer on the back of this paper.

Sweetheart Blends

Write each missing blend.
Find the words in the puzzle.

_____uck

_____ed

_____ock

_____um

c	l	o	c	k	r	t
r	v	s	d	r	u	m
a	j	f	r	o	g	s
b	s	l	e	d	k	n
j	t	a	s	f	h	a
m	a	g	s	p	a	i
t	r	u	c	k	p	l

_____ab

_____ag

_____ar

_____ail

_____og

_____ess

Name _____

Sweets and Treats

Count. Color to complete the graph.

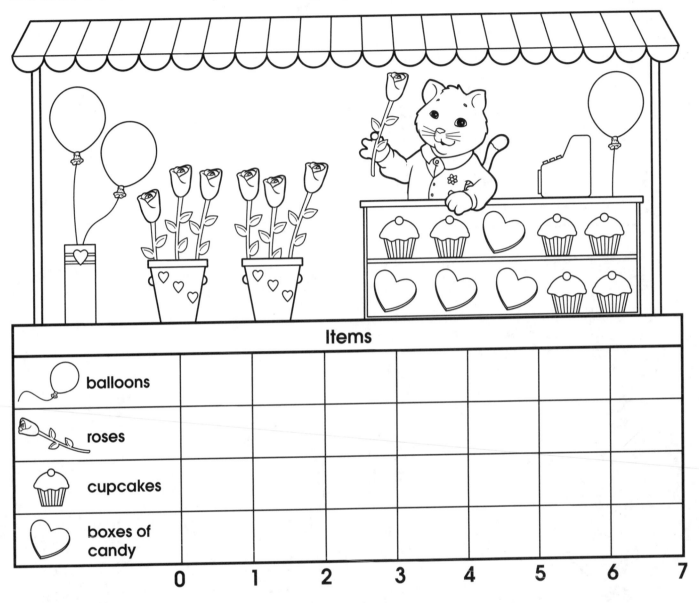

Answer the questions.

1. How many boxes of candy are there? _____

2. Are there more balloons or cupcakes? _____

3. How many more roses than balloons are there? _____

4. How many more roses than cupcakes are there? _____

Puppy Love

Add or subtract.
Color by the code.

Color Code

6, 7, or 8 — yellow
9, 10, or 11 — red
12, 13, or 14 — purple

Mimi,
Be mine
Max

A.
$$8$$
$$+\ 5$$

B.
$$13$$
$$-\ 5$$

C.
$$9$$
$$+\ 5$$

D.
$$14$$
$$-\ 5$$

E.
$$12$$
$$-\ 3$$

F.
$$9$$
$$+\ 3$$

G.
$$10$$
$$-\ 4$$

H.
$$6$$
$$+\ 4$$

I.
$$7$$
$$+\ 4$$

J.
$$11$$
$$-\ 4$$

K.
$$14$$
$$-\ 7$$

L.
$$7$$
$$+\ 7$$

Bonus Box: Max has 11 pieces of candy. He gives 6 pieces to Mimi. How many pieces of candy does Max have left? Solve this problem on the back of this paper.

"Valen-Time"

Cut and glue to match.

Color the clock
that is closest to
your bedtime.

| 8:30 |
| 10:30 |
| 9:00 |
| 3:00 |
| 7:00 |
| 12:30 |
| 12:00 |
| 4:00 |
| 2:30 |
| 7:30 |

Name _____

Read About Presidents' Day!

Look at the table of contents.

Table of Contents

George Washington 3

Abraham Lincoln 10

Birthdays........................... 17

The Flag............................ 19

The United States 22

Circle.

1. On what page do you find out about Abraham Lincoln? 10 22

2. On what page do you find out about the flag? 3 19

3. What is on page 3?   Birthdays   George Washington

4. What is on page 22?   The United States   The Flag

5. Which comes first?   The United States   George Washington

Big Book of Monthly Reproducibles • ©The Mailbox® Books • TEC61231

Add It Up, Abe!

```
   3          5          6          1
   4          1          1          2
 + 1        + 4        + 2        + 3
 ____       ____       ____       ____


   4          8          3          2
   4          2          1          7
 + 2        + 2        + 5        + 1
 ____       ____       ____       ____


   7          2          1          9
   4          3          9          0
 + 0        + 5        + 2        + 3
 ____       ____       ____       ____


              8          5          4
              3          5          2
            + 1        + 0        + 6
            ____       ____       ____
```

Bonus Box: On the back of this sheet, add your age and the ages of 2 friends.

Flyin' Fractions

Read and color.

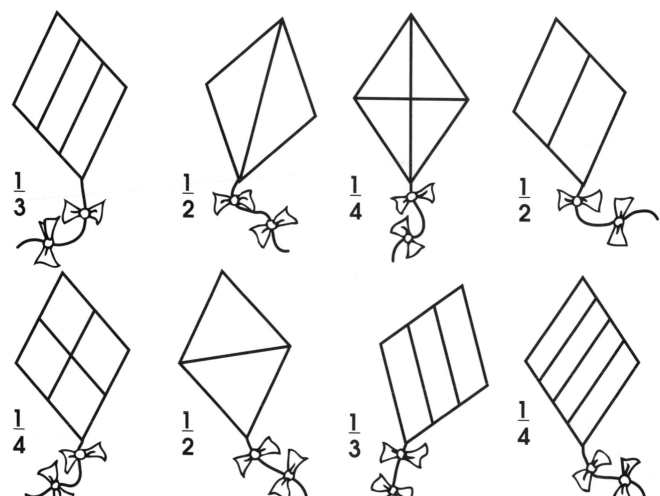

What fraction of each kite is colored?
Write.

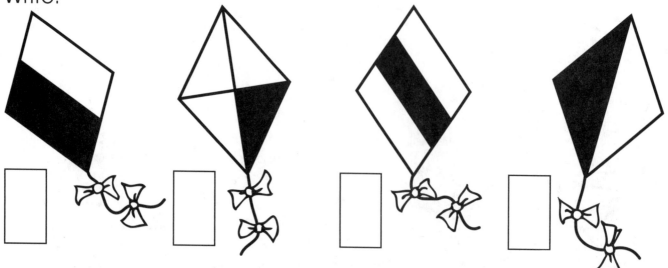

Big Book of Monthly Reproducibles • ©The Mailbox® Books • TEC61231

The "Mane" Event

Name each picture.
Cut and glue each picture beside its matching vowel.

mane	ā			
five	ī			
bone	ō			
cube	ū			

Out on a Limb

Write the contraction for each pair of words.

1. does   not   _doesn't_____

2. is   not   _____

3. was   not   _____

4. have   not   _____

5. did   not   _____

6. were   not   _____

7. do   not   _____

8. has   not   _____

9. could   not   _____

10. would   not   _____

Big Book of Monthly Reproducibles • ©The Mailbox® Books • TEC61231

Name_____

Marching In

March

Sunday	Monday	Tuesday	Wednesday	Thursday	Friday	Saturday

Write in the dates for this month.
Write the answer to each question.

1. How many days are in this month?_____

2. How many Mondays are in this month? _____

3. On what day does the month begin? _____

4. What day is March 10 on? _____

5. What day is today? _____

6. What is the date on the second Thursday? _____

Name_____

"Dandy-lions" and Lambs

Subtract.

8
−4
e

10
−1
s

9
−3
w

5
−3
l

4
−4
r

10
−2
i

11
−1
n

11
−4
t

6
−1
c

7
−4
o

12
−0
p

5
−4
m

12
−1
g

To find the message, match the letter of each answer to a line below.

			,							
2	4	7	9	6	4	2	5	3	1	4

9	12	0	8	10	11

Mighty Mushroom

Write **sh, th, ch,** or **wh.**
Color by the code.

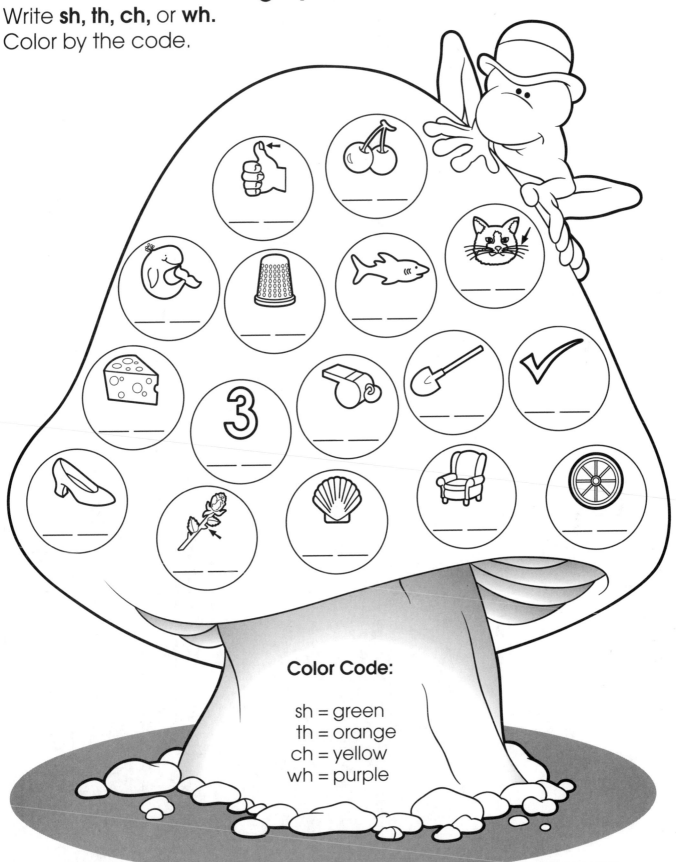

Color Code:

sh = green
th = orange
ch = yellow
wh = purple

Bonus Box: On the back of this sheet, draw two pictures of words that *end* with **sh** and **ch.**

Super Shamrock!

Cut.
Glue each sentence on the matching box.

Opinion

Fact

Bonus Box: On the back of this page, write one fact and one opinion about school.

It is fun to wear green on St. Patrick's Day.	Shamrocks have three leaves.
Shamrocks have a pretty shape.	Leprechauns wear cute clothes.
St. Patrick's Day is on March 17.	Shamrocks are plants.

Name _____

Shamrock Clocks

Write the time below each
    clock.

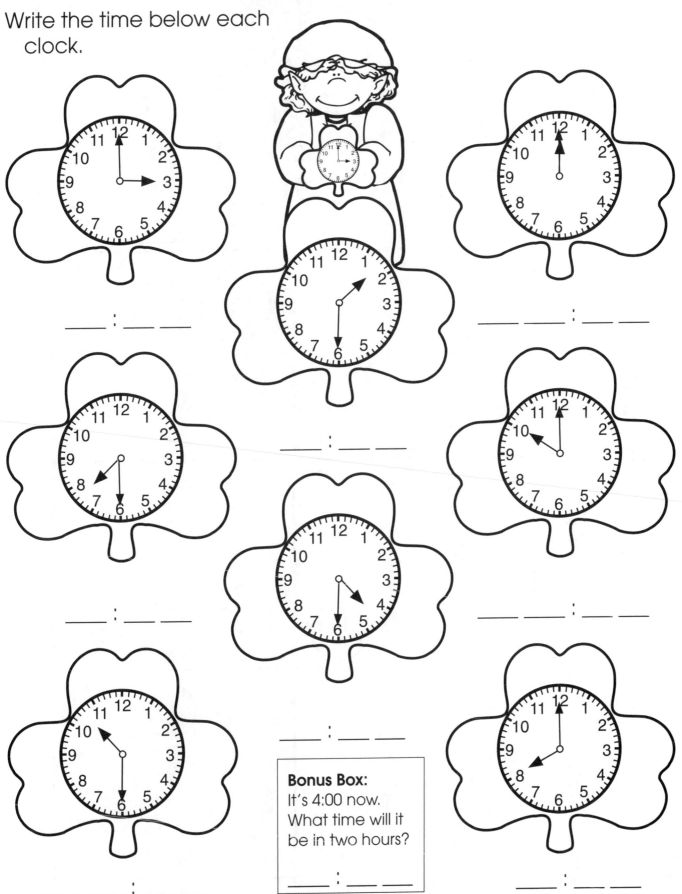

___ : ___ ___   ___ : ___ ___

___ : ___ ___   ___ : ___ ___

___ : ___ ___   ___ : ___ ___

Bonus Box:
It's 4:00 now.
What time will it
be in two hours?

___ : ___ ___

___ : ___ ___   ___ : ___ ___

A Lucky Day

Write each amount.
Color the matching coin in the pot of gold.

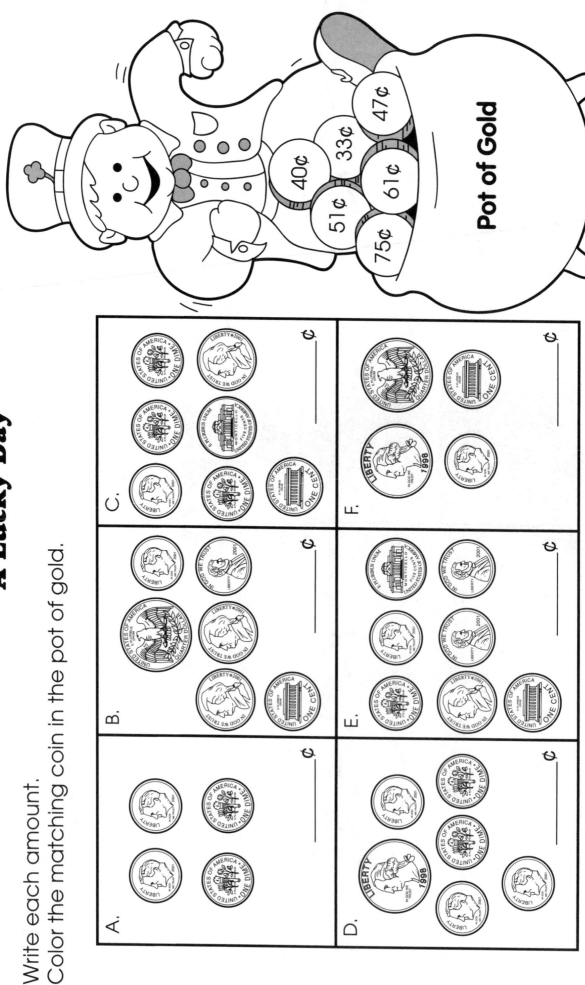

Pot of Gold

40¢ 33¢ 47¢

51¢ 61¢

75¢

A. _____ ¢

B. _____ ¢

C. _____ ¢

D. _____ ¢

E. _____ ¢

F. _____ ¢

Lucky Day

Add or subtract.

Lucky Sam had 10 coins. He found 5 more. How many coins does Sam have now? _____ coins	There were 15 shamrocks. Jake took 4. How many shamrocks are left? _____ shamrocks

There were 13 mushrooms.
A rabbit ate 3.
How many mushrooms are
   left?
 	
_____ mushrooms
	There were 9 potatoes in the
	   pot.
	3 were taken out.
	How many potatoes are left?
	
	_____ potatoes

Erin saw 6 leprechauns.
Kelly saw 7 leprechauns.
How many leprechauns did
   they both see?
 	
_____ leprechauns
	Megan bought 8 lucky
	   charms.
	Her dad gave her 2.
	How many charms does she
	   have now?
	
	_____ charms

Write the number sentence.

Patrick saw 3 pots of gold.
He saw 10 more.
How many pots of gold did he see?

Name_____

Spring Flowers

 Cut. Glue to make rhyming pairs.

Spring in Bloom

Write.

Things That
Grow

Spring makes
me feel...

I know it's
spring when...

The Windiest
Day Ever

My Amazing
Garden

On rainy spring
days, I...

Spring is the
best time for...

Fact Family Tree

Write each answer.

9 + 7 = _____

7 + 9 = _____

16 – 9 = _____

16 – 7 = _____

6 + 7 = _____

7 + 6 = _____

13 – 6 = _____

13 – 7 = _____

4 + 8 = _____

8 + 4 = _____

12 – 4 = _____

12 – 8 = _____

8 + 7 = _____

7 + 8 = _____

15 – 7 = _____

15 – 8 = _____

5 + 7 = _____

7 + 5 = _____

12 – 5 = _____

12 – 7 = _____

Bonus Box: On the back of this sheet, write four facts for this number family: 5, 6, 11.

You Can't Fool Me!

Put the words in ABC order.
Write a 1, 2, 3, or 4 by each word.

_____ bee
_____ toe
_____ land

_____ zoo
_____ feed
_____ plant

_____ see
_____ land
_____ help

_____ duck
_____ red
_____ apple

_____ goat
_____ egg
_____ cup

_____ moon
_____ bug
_____ run

_____ fall
_____ open
_____ bone
_____ queen

_____ jar
_____ color
_____ man
_____ under

_____ king
_____ ride
_____ down
_____ happy

Bonus Box: Choose one of the words above. Write it on the back of this page. Then write one word that comes before it and one word that comes after it in ABC order.

Jester's Joke

Draw an **X** on the mistake in each pattern.
Draw the correct pattern.

1.

2.

3.

4. ◯ ▢ ▢ ◯ ▢ ▢ ◯ ◯ ▢

5. △ △ ◯ △ △ ◯ ◯ △ ◯

A Graph of Goodies

Color.
Count the jelly beans. Write the totals.
Finish the graph.

Totals	
red	
yellow	
green	
orange	
blue	

	red	yellow	green	orange	blue
7					
6					
5					
4					
3					
2					
1					

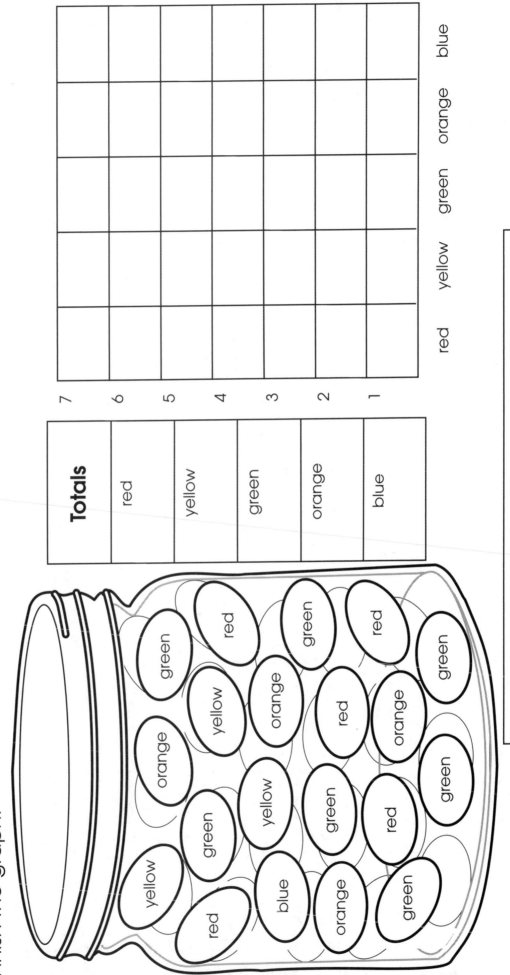

Bonus Box: On the back of this sheet, write three sentences about your graph.

Big Book of Monthly Reproducibles • ©The Mailbox® Books • TEC61231

101

All Ears

Look at each pair of words.
Color the circle beside the correct spelling.
Cut and glue to match the pictures.

○ chain
○ chayn

○ hai
○ hay

○ paint
○ paynt

○ rain
○ rayn

○ plai
○ play

○ craion
○ crayon

○ snail
○ snayl

○ nail
○ nayl

○ train
○ trayn

○ sprai
○ spray

Name _____

Bunny Funnies

Read each riddle.
Write the correct word.
Color the egg to match.

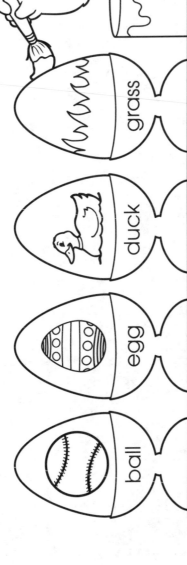

ball	egg	duck	grass	sun	flower

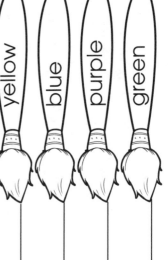

orange brown yellow blue purple green

1. I can swim. I have wings. _____

2. I am round. I am a toy. _____

3. I am hot and very bright. _____

4. I can crack. I have a shell. _____

5. I have a stem and leaves. _____

6. I can grow fast. I am green. _____

Name _____

Bunny's Delight

Add or subtract.

6 + 8 = ____   14 − 5 = ____   15 − 7 = ____

6 + 6 = ____   11 − 3 = ____   13 − 6 = ____   5 + 8 = ____

14 − 6 = ____   9 + 4 = ____   6 + 9 = ____   12 − 4 = ____

5 + 7 = ____   13 − 9 = ____   3 + 8 = ____   15 − 9 = ____

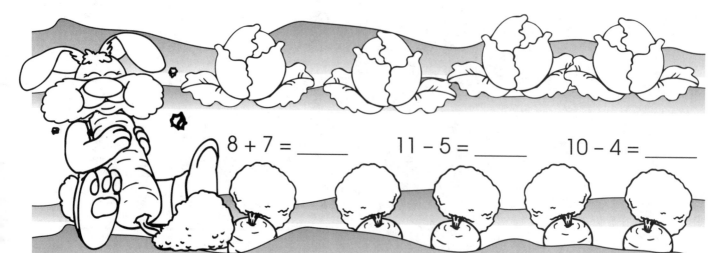

8 + 7 = ____   11 − 5 = ____   10 − 4 = ____

Taking Care of the Earth

Read.
Circle the bold words.
Write the contraction.
Use the word bank to help you.

1. **We are** taking care of the earth. _____

2. **We will** plant trees. _____

3. **It is** good to pick up litter. _____

4. **She will** turn off the lights. _____

5. **Who is** taking a bike instead of a car? _____

6. **Let us** recycle cardboard boxes! _____

7. **They have** been recycling newspapers. _____

8. **You are** a friend of the earth! _____

Word Bank

Let's	She'll
Who's	They've
We'll	We're
It's	You're

Earth Pals

Add **s** or **es**.

box_____

can_____

glass_____

light_____

park_____

bus_____

shower_____

bush_____

Use the words above to complete the sentences.

1. Take _____ instead of baths.

2. Plant trees and _____.

3. Take _____ instead of cars.

4. Recycle soda _____.

5. Turn off the _____ when you leave a room.

6. Recycle cardboard _____.

7. Pick up litter in the _____.

8. Drink from _____ instead of cans.

Bonus Box: On the back of this paper, write the word *beach*. Add **s** or **es.** Then use the word in a sentence.

A Week's Worth of Rain

It has rained for five days.
A **rain gauge** measured the rainfall
each day.

Monday	Tuesday	Wednesday	Thursday	Friday
6 5 4 3 2 1 inches	6 5 4 3 2 1 inches	6 5 4 3 2 1 inches	6 5 4 3 2 1 inches	6 5 4 3 2 1 inches

Write or circle to answer each question. Use the graph.

1. On what day did it rain the most? _____

2. How many inches of rain fell on Friday?

    4 inches   5 inches   6 inches

3. Which day got more rain than Monday but less rain than
Friday? _____

4. Which day got the least amount of rain?

    Monday   Wednesday   Friday

5. Which two days got the same amount of rain?

_____ and _____

6. How much rain fell during all five days? _____ inches

Name _____

Puddle Practice

Add.
Glue each raindrop above its sum.
Glue the extra raindrop on the back of this sheet.
Write the sum.

6   15   14

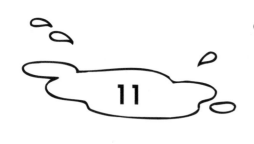  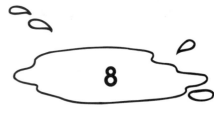

11   12   8

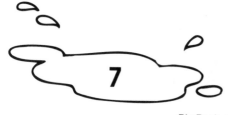  

7   9   10

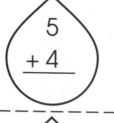 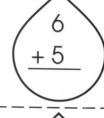

$8 + 4$	$3 + 7$	$5 + 4$	$6 + 5$	$8 + 0$
$4 + 3$	$2 + 4$	$9 + 5$	$7 + 8$	$5 + 8$

Colorful Clouds

Color each cloud that has two equal parts.

Rainbow Delight

Write > or < between each pair of clouds.
The first one has been done for you.

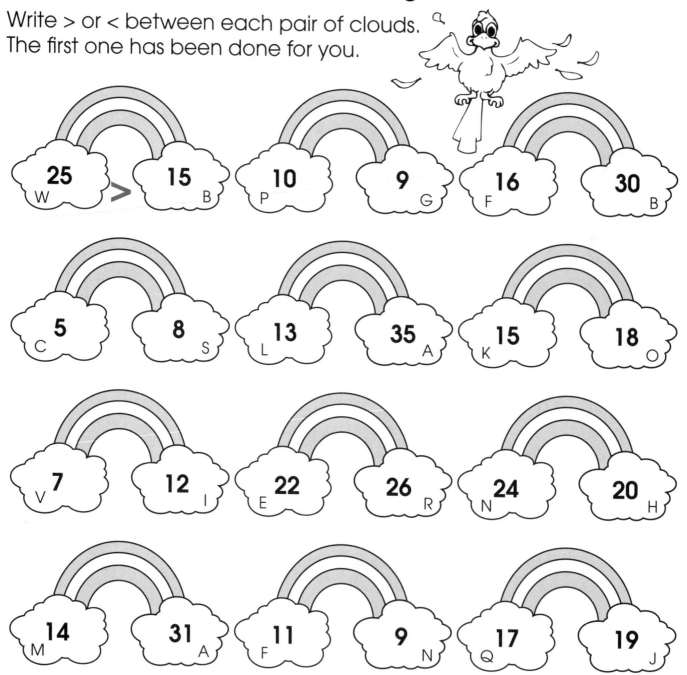

To solve the riddle, match the letters of the greater numbers to the lines.
Some numbers will not be used.

What kind of bow is hard to tie?

——— ——— —— —— —— —— —— ——
35   26   31   12   24   30   18   25

Big Book of Monthly Reproducibles • ©The Mailbox® Books • TEC61231

Night Melodies

Antonyms are words that have
opposite meanings.
Cut and glue to match.

cold	

over	

day	

yes	

open	

new	

slow	

up	

hard	

before	

fast	no	under	hot	after
old	night	soft	down	close

Name _____

Snacktime

Synonyms are words that have
the same meanings.
Write a synonym for each word.
Use the word bank.

Word Bank
fast   smile
pretty   small
wet   friend
glad

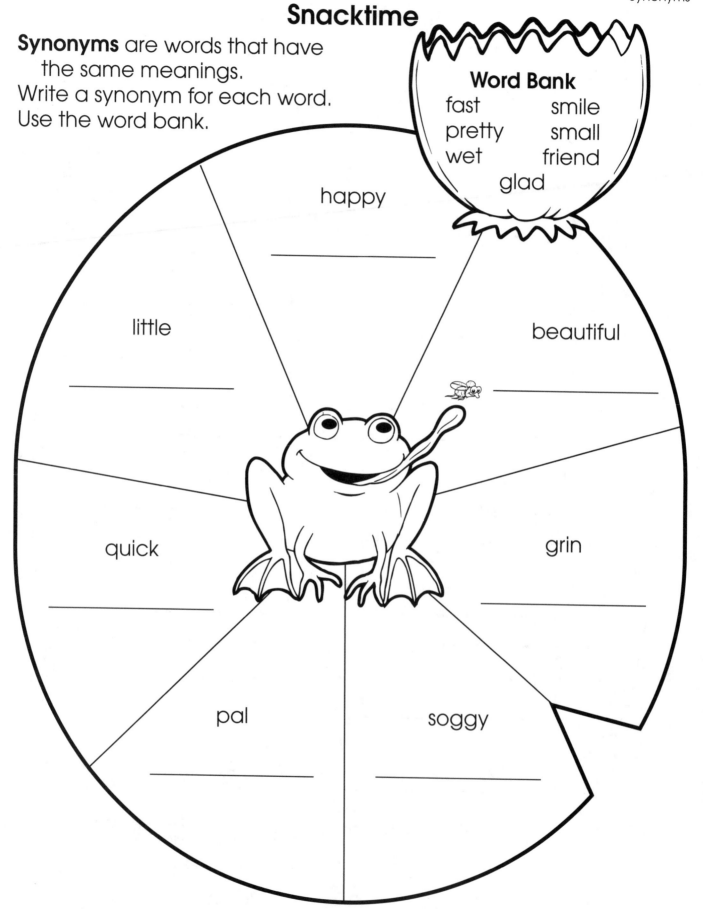

happy
_____

little
_____

beautiful
_____

quick
_____

grin
_____

pal
_____

soggy
_____

Follow the Leaper

Add or subtract.
Color by the code.

Color Code
0–7 — yellow
8–16 — green

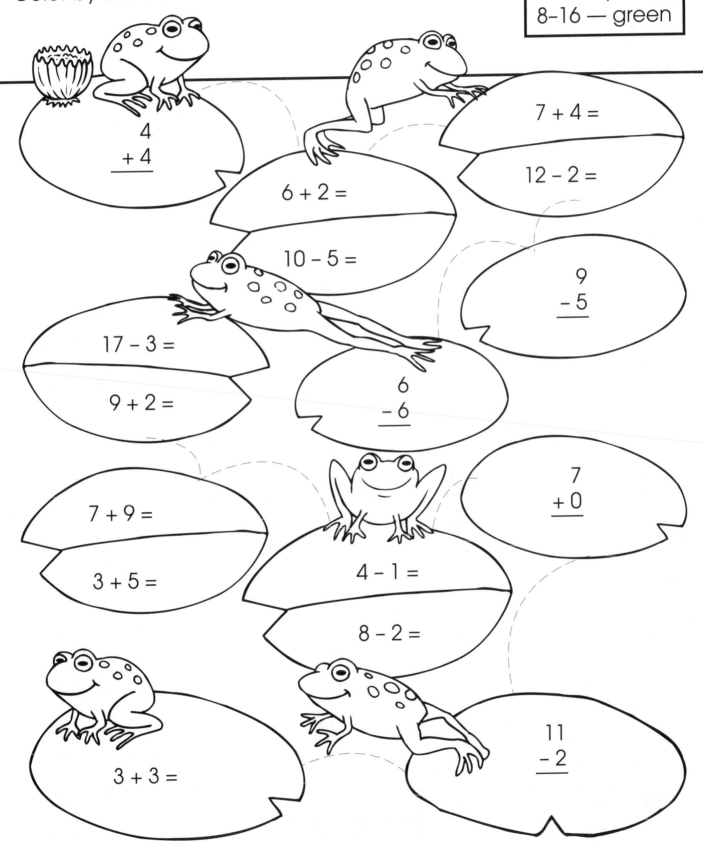

$$4 + 4$$

$$7 + 4 =$$

$$6 + 2 =$$

$$12 - 2 =$$

$$10 - 5 =$$

$$9 - 5$$

$$17 - 3 =$$

$$6 - 6$$

$$9 + 2 =$$

$$7 + 0$$

$$7 + 9 =$$

$$3 + 5 =$$

$$4 - 1 =$$

$$8 - 2 =$$

$$3 + 3 =$$

$$11 - 2$$

Batter Up!

Say each word.
Listen for syllables.
Write the number of syllables beside
each word.

_____ ball

_____ slide

_____ batter

_____ lineup

_____ strike

_____ outfield

_____ equipment

_____ double

_____ bases

_____ coach

_____ bunt

_____ error

_____ baseball

_____ manager

_____ throw

_____ hit

_____ glove

_____ game

_____ pitcher

_____ out

Bonus Box: If a word has more than one syllable, draw a line (or lines) to divide the syllables. Example: bat/ter

Big Book of Monthly Reproducibles • ©The Mailbox® Books • TEC61231

Who's Winning?

Scoreboard

Inning	1	2	3	4	5	6	7	8	9	Total Runs
Bats	0	2	1	3	0	2	1	0	2	
Stars	1	0	1	0	2	1	3	0	4	

Answer each question.
Use the scoreboard.

1. Which team scored more runs in the 4th inning? _____

2. Which team scored 2 runs in the 6th inning? _____

3. How many runs did the Bats score in the 2nd inning? _____

4. How many runs did the Stars score in the 5th inning? _____

5. In what inning did both teams score 1 run? _____

6. How many runs did the Bats score in innings 1 and 2? _____

Bonus Box: Add each team's scores for all nine innings. Write the total score for each team at the end of the scoreboard. Circle the winning team's name on the scoreboard.

Big Book of Monthly Reproducibles • ©The Mailbox® Books • TEC61231

Name_____

Fiesta Fun

Read each problem.
Solve.
Write the answer.

9 **mariachi** play.
2 walk away.
How many
are left? _____

8 **piñatas** hang in the shop.
4 more are hung.
How many in all? _____

5 **sombreros** are sold.
6 more are sold.
How many
are sold? _____

11 **maracas** make noise.
4 more make noise.
How many in all? _____

7 **flowers** are in the vase.
6 more are put in the vase.
How many in all? _____

10 **tacos** are on the plate.
4 are eaten.
How many are left? _____

12 **peppers** are in the jar.
3 are eaten.
How many are left? _____

13 **children** watch the parade.
5 go away.
How many
are left? _____

Bonus Box: Circle the biggest answer. Make a box around the smallest answer.

Big Book of Monthly Reproducibles • ©The Mailbox® Books • TEC61231

Rows of Roses

Write.
Use the word bank.
Color by the code.

Color Code

o_e as in **bone**
—orange

oa as in **boat**
—yellow

Word Bank

soap	goat	coat	road
cone	hose	note	rope

Bonus Box: On the back of this page, write two sentences that each have at least one word with the long-*o* sound.

Planting Plan

Cut and glue in order.

1	2	3	4	5

Add water.

Cover the seeds with dirt.

Dig a hole.

Watch the plant grow.

Put in the seeds.

Name_____

Potted Plants

Write the missing addend for each problem.
Use the flower to help you.

$$\begin{array}{r} 8 \\ + \square \\ \hline 12 \end{array}$$

$$\begin{array}{r} 6 \\ + \square \\ \hline 9 \end{array}$$

$$\begin{array}{r} \square \\ + 3 \\ \hline 8 \end{array}$$

$$\begin{array}{r} \square \\ + 4 \\ \hline 11 \end{array}$$

$$\begin{array}{r} 9 \\ + \square \\ \hline 12 \end{array}$$

$$\begin{array}{r} \square \\ + 2 \\ \hline 7 \end{array}$$

$$\begin{array}{r} 7 \\ + \square \\ \hline 8 \end{array}$$

$$\begin{array}{r} \square \\ + 4 \\ \hline 9 \end{array}$$

$$\begin{array}{r} \square \\ + 5 \\ \hline 10 \end{array}$$

Busy Bees

Add a period at the end of each complete sentence.
Cut.
Glue.

Bonus Box: On the back of this sheet, write three more complete sentences about bees.

Big Book of Monthly Reproducibles • ©The Mailbox® Books • TEC61231

Bees make honey

The worker bees

Is good to eat

In a hive

The queen bee lays eggs

One queen lives in a hive

Worker bees clean the hive

A lot of honey

Honey is sweet

Name _____

"Un-bee-lievable!"

Look at each picture.
Color the flower beside the sentence that tells what will probably
 happen next.

⚘ The dog sleeps.

⚘ The dog chews the bone.

⚘ The dog chases a cat.

⚘ The girl rides her bike.

⚘ The girl swings.

⚘ The girl reads the book.

⚘ The boy eats lunch.

⚘ The boy plays ball.

⚘ The boy runs.

⚘ The bird flies away.

⚘ The bird makes a nest.

⚘ The bird feeds the baby birds.

⚘ The girl cooks.

⚘ The girl blows out the candles.

⚘ The girl goes home.

Bonus Box: On the back of this sheet, write a story about one of the pictures.

All Abuzz!

Read each word.
Color each flower with a noun yellow.
Color each flower without a noun orange.

Remember:
A **noun** is a person, a place, or a thing.

bee

garden

see

hive

eggs

sit

job

in

fast

flower

yellow

honey

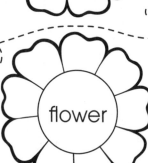

wing

pretty

insect

queen

Bonus Box: Write six more nouns on the back of this sheet.

Buzzing Into Addition

Add.
Color by the code.

$$9 \\ +3$$

$$9 \\ +6$$

$$5 \\ +7$$

$$4 \\ +8$$

$$9 \\ +7$$

$$9 \\ +9$$

$$7 \\ +8$$

$$7 \\ +9$$

$$8 \\ +4$$

$$8 \\ +7$$

$$7 \\ +5$$

$$6 \\ +6$$

$$8 \\ +8$$

$$6 \\ +9$$

$$3 \\ +9$$

Color Code

12 = purple   15 = orange   16 = yellow   18 = red

Bonus Box: On the back of this sheet, write an addition word problem with the numbers 8 and 4.

America Remembers

Read.

The last Monday in May is a special day. It is Memorial Day. It is a day to think about the people who died in wars. A lot of towns have parades. Some people play in bands. Some people put out flags. It is a day to thank all soldiers.

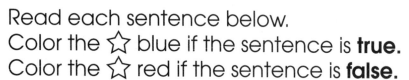

Read each sentence below.
Color the ☆ blue if the sentence is **true.**
Color the ☆ red if the sentence is **false.**

 1. Memorial Day is in March.

 2. Memorial Day is on a Tuesday.

 3. You may see a lot of flags on Memorial Day.

 4. There are parades on Memorial Day.

 5. It is a day to think about soldiers.

Bonus Box: On the back of this paper, write a sentence that tells one way that you may celebrate Memorial Day. Draw a picture to go with it.

Name_____

Poppies for Sale!

Poppies and Memorial Day go together. Volunteers sell these small red flowers on Memorial Day. The money from these sales helps disabled veterans. Sometimes Memorial Day is even called Poppy Day.

Add.
Color the poppy with the matching sum.

$$
\begin{array}{r} 3 \\ 6 \\ +\,4 \\ \hline \end{array}
\qquad
\begin{array}{r} 5 \\ 4 \\ +\,7 \\ \hline \end{array}
\qquad
\begin{array}{r} 1 \\ 8 \\ +\,5 \\ \hline \end{array}
\qquad
\begin{array}{r} 2 \\ 4 \\ +\,3 \\ \hline \end{array}
$$

$$
\begin{array}{r} 8 \\ 9 \\ +\,0 \\ \hline \end{array}
\qquad
\begin{array}{r} 2 \\ 9 \\ +\,4 \\ \hline \end{array}
\qquad
\begin{array}{r} 8 \\ 8 \\ +\,2 \\ \hline \end{array}
\qquad
\begin{array}{r} 5 \\ 3 \\ +\,4 \\ \hline \end{array}
$$

$$
\begin{array}{r} 6 \\ 2 \\ +\,3 \\ \hline \end{array}
\qquad
\begin{array}{r} 1 \\ 7 \\ +\,2 \\ \hline \end{array}
\qquad
\begin{array}{r} 2 \\ 5 \\ +\,3 \\ \hline \end{array}
\qquad
\begin{array}{r} 7 \\ 6 \\ +\,5 \\ \hline \end{array}
$$

16   15   13   9   17   10

18   14   12   10   18   11

Name_____

First-Grade Days

Read.

Reading, writing, math, and more,

I worked hard, that's for sure!

Learning new things in fun ways,

I'll remember my first-grade days!

Complete each sentence.

I am glad I learned _____

_____

The best book I read this year was _____

_____

My favorite class activity was _____

_____

I liked it when _____

_____

Bonus Box: On the back of this sheet, draw and color a picture that shows a favorite memory from the past year. Write about the memory.

Name _____

Field Day Fun

GRADE 1

GO TEAM

Read.
Decide if you must add or subtract.
Write the math sentence.

A. 8 ants run races.
4 more join in.
How many ants run in all?

◯ ____ ____ = ____ ants

B. 15 ants run on the track.
6 ants stop to rest.
How many ants do not rest?

◯ ____ ____ = ____ ants

C. 13 ants toss beanbags.
7 ants get the beanbags in the basket.
How many ants do not?

◯ ____ ____ = ____ ants

D. 9 ants throw red balls.
9 ants throw yellow balls.
How many balls are thrown in all?

◯ ____ ____ = ____ balls

E. 11 ants run through the tires.
10 ants fall down.
How many ants do not fall?

◯ ____ ____ = ____ ants

F. 14 ants run races.
2 ants jump rope.
How many ants are there in all?

◯ ____ ____ = ____ ants

Bonus Box: On the back of this paper, draw the field day activity that you like the most. Then write a math problem to go with your drawing.

Big Book of Monthly Reproducibles • ©The Mailbox® Books • TEC61231

Fun in the Sun

Add.

A. 8
2
+3
___

B. 9
4
+5
___

C. 6
5
+7
___

D. 5
6
+0
___

E. 1
4
+9
___

F. 6
3
+3
___

G. 3
2
+2
___

H. 4
5
+1
___

I. 7
2
+8
___

J. 1
3
+9
___

K. 4
6
+1
___

L. 0
8
+8
___